Home by Dark

Also by Pam Brown

Books
Sureblock
Cocabola's Funny Picture Book
Automatic Sad
Cafe Sport
Correspondences
Country & Eastern
Small Blue View
Selected Poems 1971-1982
Keep It Quiet
New & Selected Poems
This World. This Place
50 - 50
Text thing
Dear Deliria
True Thoughts
Authentic Local

Chapbooks
Little Droppings
My Lightweight Intentions
Drifting topoi
eleven 747 poems
Let's Get Lost (with Ken Bolton & Laurie Duggan)
Peel Me A Zibibbo
farout_library_software (with Maged Zaher)
In my phone
Anyworld
More than a feuilleton

e-book
the meh of z z z z

Pamphlets
Montréal
Train train
Sentimental

Theatre
As Much Trouble As Talking (with Jan McKemmish)

Home by Dark

Pam Brown

Shearsman Books

First published in the United Kingdom in 2013 by
Shearsman Books Ltd
50 Westons Hill Drive
Emersons Green
BRISTOL
BS16 7DF

Shearsman Books Ltd Registered Office
30–31 St. James Place, Mangotsfield, Bristol BS16 9JB
(this address not for correspondence)

www.shearsman.com

ISBN 978-1-84861-288-4

Copyright © Pam Brown, 2013

The right of Pam Brown to be identified as the author
of this work has been asserted by her in accordance with the
Copyrights, Designs and Patents Act of 1988.
All rights reserved.

Thanks to Melbourne-based artist Jon Cattapan for his generosity in
allowing the reproduction of a detail from his painting
'Atonal Group Study 2' for this book's cover.

Contents

I
Windows wound down	9
Holiday Guide to Everything	17
Wet flannelette	19
Country Town	21
In Queensland	24
Powdery	25
Like 1988	26

II
Femininny	31
1995	34
Half life	37
American Memories, Melbourne	38
A Mo th of Sundays	43
Zottegem	45
The southern of someplace	51

III
Opportunities	55
Rehab for Everyone	56
Spirulina to go	59
No Worries	65
Leaving the World	69
Living	72
Haywire here	73

IV
Dry ice	81
Seriously	84
A moving cloud	86
In my phone	93

Nina Hagen	96
What's the frequency, Kenneth?	98
Closed on Mondays	101

V

Worldless	109
Feed the orchid	115
iNext twilight	117
All fuelled out	118
A day late	119
Sugar tube	121
More than a feuilleton	124
Acknowledgements	131

I

Just keep staring into that English-language night sky.
KEVIN DAVIES

Windows wound down

parked under
a chalky old light pole,
windows wound down,
dozing on the front seat,
on the radio
Chinese classical music

hot night tonight,
across the road
a man is wearing
his hat, indoors.

the stars that I love,
when I remember
to look at them,
blink above the building

*

I've memorised
a Keats sonnet
for February
a Tom Clark poem
for March

&
julienned the carrots
for spicy carrots
with harissa, cumin,
parsley, garlic, lemon,
while listening
to crazy music—
Albert Ayler

*

a Czech poetry paperback
bought in 1971,
there's a 30 cent ticket
to the Penguin Reserve
on Phillip Island
and a poignant note
tucked between the pages
of a poem marked with a pencilled 'x'

'x'—Vladimir Holan, Changes—
This is our hope : that we have passed
the limits of the last reality.
But while consciousness disappears
it is the very consciousness
whose constant changes
remain…

the note—
P
I can't bring myself to write
what's in my head
I am splitting up north I guess
I love you
B

*

The Collected Poems
of Gwen Harwood
is on the table
but I should
prepare a talk
for Zines in April

*

going on online,
a small discussion
(between 3 poets)
about experimental poetry
and free verse that one poet says
is really
anecdotal 'sincerity'
wrapped up in the unified 'I'

oh dear I think that must mean me,
with whom I am definitely stuck,
I have
my limitations, though
not always 'sincere',
and never 'unified'—
only paranoid

*

do carpenters
read novels
about carpenters?
do pastrycooks
about pastrycooks?
poets read novels
by poets,
like
Roberto Bolaño

yes, it seems so

*

another phone call
more cancer
and another
a month later

like Michael said,
now we'll spend
the rest of our lives
watching our friends die.

*

End of the First Week

*

by the time they caught Karadzic
everyone here had forgotten
who he was, what he'd done

*

water on mars ?
let's fuck mars up too

space terrain
flag a claim,
space fear sphere,
see you tomorrow

*

why not
recalibrate your lifestyle

how <u>did</u> Jean Genet
live in hotels
for so long?

*

she wiped her face
with the wettex
then turned to kiss me

let me
track your parcel
darling

*

find a city,
well, find a city first, I agree,
find myself a city to live in.
David Byrne, Cities

I can't google-map my past,
where we lived is classified

*

cept
f u Peter P !
u know y

*

walk the spoodle
and the labradoodle

past the pot of pesto
under the patio gas heater

grown men
with ridiculous dogs

*

End of the Second Week

*

the podiatrist's fingertips
are orange with nicotine,
my corn recoils

*

lithium eclipse
a new cocktail

ice wine
a minor fever

*

booking in to
the Nasty Uncles Hotel
one moonlit night,
a double-bed room,
a mean argument,
a bus stop

*

the first Koreans of the season,
cloth hats, one silver coolie,
comic-print backpacks,
peering over fences at plants
imported from Korea—

it's Spring

*

End of the Third Week

*

gone solar

*

cicadas sucking sap
underground—
that's optimism

*

I'm not going
to Zines in April,
too old too tired too late

but

still in opposition—
dead prepositions,
and needless adverbs

*

industrialising pollination

my white paper poem
has
no conclusion

I would like to see
some viridian,
in my opinion
a neglected colour

   *

End of the Month

Holiday Guide to Everything

thin thread,
spider strokes a fly,
weak sunlight on a tree

the ratio of frequencies—
yellowish green
with pink edges

I'm indoors
scrubbing grime
from stainless steel ridges
on the draining sink

recessions don't stop
for Sunday

don't open the door
don't answer the phone
we need nothing

the wind
has blown the devil
and the dog uphill

fog ascends
round the catchment area,
water seeps under the tor

on the highway
a weird tree stump
in a cage—
The Explorers' Tree

some pioneer
tried to understand
the everywhen,
blackfella time

but me,
I wait
long hours,
even years

meanwhile

the jury plays sudoku,
short sentence dreaming

Joe Henderson
beams lasers at the high notes

satellites police the stars

sesame seeds stick
in a tooth socket

acquit me of my consternation,
is this my holiday ?

pollination is a dying art

the dead princess's car wreck
up for auction

Wet flannelette

who are those people
running on my grass?

*

dragging the wheely bin
to the footpath,
a shooting star
zim   a flash
above the dark pathway
at the back of the house

through the window
little green standby lights
on the computer equipment—
the cat burglar's runway

it's a carbon toe-print
in there

*

empty street
in a couch potato smalltown,
every human indoors
in home-entertainment

*

flagpole
in a bare yard

*

the best rubbish
behind
the buildings—
cardboard boxes,
twisted wire,
wet carpet, wet flannelette

Country town

frisky calves
in the morning frost,
that's this nature thing,
the big cows too
are warming up,
blowing fogs of breath
between each cuddy chomp,
the sun is rising, as is steam
from wondrous and plentiful
green streams of piss

in the paddocks
along the railway line

*

hours later, after lunch,
reciting a poem—
    sheep and cows
    standing for hours
    beneath the boughs—
to half a dozen
variously demented elders
at the day care centre

    what is this life
    if full of care
    we have no time
    to stand and stare

corny even in memory

*

a different morning
coming back from the station
with an unused day-return ticket,
I wave, a feeble flick, to Viken,
he's in the doorway to his gallery,
opening up for the day,
I've just vomited
into some weedy shrubs
next to the garage,
so I'll miss an appointment,
this is my quotidian
but it's not everything

*

on the bus
a German backpacker
explains
'the stolen generations'
to her Dutch girlfriend,
they're carrying didgeridoos
in custom-made canvas cases

*

every morning
breaking fine spider webs
on my way to the car

*

black cockatoos
squealing and hissing
in the radiata pines up on the hill
above the Catholic church

down here
Orchestra Baobab's
'Made in Dakar'—
drowning them out
from the humid verandah

*

outside the take-away
four and twenty myna birds
scrabbling for a chip

In Queensland

hot and stonkered
cattle lying in the road
to carnarvon gorge

trudging
to the rock art
sixteen miles a day
up the gorge
and back again

cabbage tree palms
in a clearing
near the creek

headlights off
driving in moonlight
on a narrow road
dividing silver paddocks

dozing in the shade
on bribie island
in the dirty sand
under the church

in the middle of the night
we lay down drunk
under the frangipani trees
on wickham terrace

Powdery

white frost,
walls and windows
streaky with condensation

you can check your thought,
not speak,
eyelid skinflakes
spot your lenses

a cork placemat,
a 6B pencil, teeth marks,
(not yours, whose?)

you cheated yourself
of natural ageing,
ageing quickly, medication
induced,   a shadow,
a dry thin lip

bul buls peck
at the frost-dried grass,
their song

no alcohol,
weak sunlight, powdery
through a dirty pane

not didactic,
how can you continue
to learn?

Like 1988

my arm around your shoulder
                we walked downhill

from Forbes Street
                towards Bourke

then I saw you
                on the opposite side of the street,

at the lights
                you waved,

I raised my hand from your shoulder
                        and waved back

your hair coloured
                with coppery streaks

      you looked self-engaged, distant,

as if we weren't

I touched your waist,
                your dress fluted, like paper,
white and red

                    you
    so strong
                it seemed like 1988

walking with you on a walk
                towards you

later, you were fixing a bicycle,
the carrier on the rear
above the wheel,

you deflected me

we had
already been together

time apart
or lost

was something lost?

II

I'm committed to my artform as a lifetime journey.
                                                         Nicole Kidman

Me too.
        Funny Papa Smith

Femininny

fixed sensations

*

can't hang
a hoya
crooked
on a fence

nor
a nodding violet
and
a chain of hearts

*

from may to june
monosyllabic
months
don't work

not
for titles

except,
maybe,
may '68,
it's
the '68
isn't it?

gathering
nuts in may,

it's
the polysemy,
nuts

    *

fishy sensations

    *

quality
vocal
live set

chansons
to me

dearest ancient
free-to-air
fossil

    *

loathing
palm ferns

disappointed
that you brought
palm ferns

    *

seasonal suckle
classified pisces

    *

eschew
christian mingle

     *

but
do not curdle
introital maiden—

you're a great idea,
a unique event,
epicene

     *

fission sensations

     *

can't hang
a pailful of fluff

rusty bolt
windy corridor

1995

the day after
the very long reading,
at the very cool venue,
we, the audience, <u>were</u>
those sluts, those girls—
rats in our hair
vampires in our anus
blood, piss, shit,
spit, bones, vomit—
Kathy Acker's
drunken girls,
she meant <u>us</u>,
that's the way she read
to us   the way
she treated us
& Carl said   hell,
I wanted to
go straight home
& pop <u>my</u> cherry.

today
Carl told me
his girlfriend
once collected
her menstrual blood
in a jar
for potential use
in an art installation
but ended up
throwing out
the jar of blood
& using molasses.

I told Carl
about a beaded
tampon curtain
someone hung
at the Yellow House
where I made a sculpture
over twenty years ago
& now I've had
menopause.
Carl made
a tiny sigh
& said   oh well
you're not even
in the culture
now   & I said
then I think
I must be
one of
Kathy Acker's
incommensurable
pirates,
not one of whom
possesses a name.

then
Carl's girlfriend
phoned to say
she had just had
a 'Lair of the White Worm'
haircut
& as he, Carl,
had only about
30 minutes work
left to do
on his Kant essay,

they would get
Eisenstein's
'Ivan the Terrible'
from Johnny Dark's
video shop
(just up the street
from my place)
to watch tonight.

soon
Carl's girlfriend
is taking him
to IntenCity,
a virtual reality
place
at Hurstville,
which might
be called
Intent City
(I don't know)
where, he said,
you can do
painless boxing.

Half life

benzene-coated
    dog and bub burb

antiques delivery van
    lumbering uphill

the past   the past
    is heritage brass

now is always
    only now

in a different time
    a swirl of concerns

the mirror in the movie
    no longer reflects

high radiation levels
    by the looks of it

starbod extasy
    caught in cactus

try ½ price
    body sculpting

turn the building
    inside out

get a half life
    or whatever's legitimate

American Memories, Melbourne
(not quite after Hope Mirrlees)

I want a panorama

SOUTH - WEST
CACAO BLOOKER
GOG & MAGOG

green art deco bakelite in the national gallery

FITZROY (ST ASPEN SHIRAZ)
BRUNSWICK (SQUAWKING MAGPIE SAUVIGNON BLANC)
PARLIAMENTARY MUSEUM (HAZELGROVE PINOT NOIR)

creak chug creak chug creak chug under Princes Bridge on the Yarra

CASTLEMAINE ROCK

Greek woman tearing the gig posters from the lightpole outside her son's bar

Going down Madam ?

follow the commemorative brass plaques in the footpath
a golden mile must be almost two kilometres

ne rien faire   walk slowly   doing nothing
for approximately two hours

WARAKURNA ARTISTS at Alcaston Gallery in Fitzroy until Saturday

discover why Melbourne is called 'marvellous'

a grey mouse running through green & purple wisteria vines

TIN BOX BUILDINGS
attached to creaking weatherboard cottages

the awful HARD art of the minimal
strikes here and
strikes again in Montréal, actually strikes TWICE in Montréal
at the Museum of Contemporary Art
and at the Musée des Beaux Arts
too !

DUCRAY ICTYANE
crème émolliente hydratante   blow wind blow
buy Magic Gloves at Dollarama

red wine and voodoo at *RUBIS ROUGE*

in the USA public toilets flush automatically which can be alarming
all announcers have Spanish accents
the L-A-N-G-U-A-G-E poetry is really realism
Ron Silliman's VOG is Voice Over Guy, Voice Of God,
Very Ordinary Glory
Vital Organs Grim ...

on the SILVER STAR 91
from Philadelphia Pennsylvania to Richmond Virginia
(Dixie Hummingbirds, Cab Calloway, Ruth Brown, Amos Milburn)

the suitcase keys
are in
the alternative medicine pill bottle

GREAT DISMAL SWAMP

Henry 'Box' Brown
mailed himself to freedom
in a big box labelled 'Dry Goods'—from Virginia to Philadelphia
in 1849

on the NORTHEAST REGIONAL 94
from Richmond Virginia to Washington District Columbia
(Elizabeth Cotten, Duke Ellington, Marvin Gaye)

innumerable   Stars & Stripes   innumerable

Famous American Female Poet :
'What you might need to know is that you might not make it
But if you do, you might have needed an astrolabe
or a two-bit smile or smirk, this is a style
that could get you a cup of coffee'

AMERICAN coffee ??

old worms in the woodwork
old hooks on the hat rack
old bottomless cups depleted

TIPPING drives me crazy -
quoted price
+Value Added Tax
+15%
bring a pocket calculator

As Portentous As The Opening Chords Of A Big Bob Dylan Ballad
the prescience of the dead

Yours truly, Your paranormal host,
Adelaide

   hooray   at last   here's the panorama   coming up now

discover all the charms of ELEGANT and CONTEMPORARY
melbourne

cross the west gate bridge for AMAZING city views
observe the yarra river's BUSTLING ACTIVITY
see queen victoria market, fitzroy gardens
and albert park, home to the australian formula one grand prix.
visit the HISTORIC shrine of remembrance
stroll along southbank's waterfront precinct

this city has it ALL — discover it for yourself

pour boire, merci, thank you, tip

taxi to lax

KOONS   RUSCHA   CHEECH the CHICANO
JaMaiCan LeMoNaDe   woo you never know
HeY HeY VLaMinCK !
Maurice Vlaminck's portrait in oilpaint of Guillaume Apollinaire

white women smiling into the air
Michael Jackson and his monkey

NO POETRY MEETING TODAY —
EVERYONE IS WORKING

greasy screen at the mex internet café grill
too dangerous

　　　　　　　　to walk south
　　　　　down the SAN DIEGO freeway

　　　Almost Completely Finished With Pop Art Finally
　　　　　　　　call the paramedics

A Mo th of Sundays

hi

hiatus

u u
i o
a e

tom verlaine's
the o of adore

ooee ooee baby
1 9 7 7

*

zot

double zot
zaps a month

zot that
sun spot
doc

sun
on some
sundays

leap year

digital calendar
flipped

somedays

*

narrow screen

sterday's
orld

iday

ormer
iberal backbencher

HE
30
ORT

nario
uthor

ustralian

*

take your ticket
and your leave

zeugma

Zottegem
although short, a saga

canal side
      no pingos

but I got
      to Zottegem

hours travelling
      in vast flatnesses

I successfully disregarded
      the landscape

in the sustenance carriage
   melted cheese
      clung limply to a pan

*

      veering tenses
dispersed
   and went coursing
      into the present -

*

the artist
   with bible syndrome's
ganglions
      need smashing

*

the corpse in the copse
    is,
      ostensibly,
down there
   in that narrow valley
filled with mist
   like a saucer of smoke

*

directions revolve,
    fooling the mind

stars seem to freeze

*

'wherever you go there you are'
    bumper sticker

taxi
   from Cronulla
      to Gunnamatta

where are you
   when
 you're right here?

where are you
       now?

*

the seeds of unhappiness
        planted
  by some glum bartender

    as you explicate
your race against the hours
   already repeated
      night after drinks
after nights

readiness,
     put simply,
         is exhausting

*

you must ignore
    your contemporaries'
claimed exceptionalisms
—
all
that intensive hoop la
     celebrating gewgaws

*

no comedy
   under a mouldy pile,
just ol' John Cage
  and his cladistic mushrooms

*

my feet,
   down there,

like Jimmy Schuyler's
    red stained toenail,
my toes, bluish
    from K-Mart bedsocks

*

spiky as a synapse,
    orange pandanus

snake in the ceiling,
    curvy as a sine wave,

there goes the jetsam,
    over the railing,
    floating down river

and, bobbing,
  a plastic beach ball

*

backpack heavy as bricks—
    not books, just burdens

jettison that biggest thing,
    you're in a hurry

fast hovercraft
    to the pink university—

tropical green lawns,
    gum shadings,
  placid poetry culture,
    (can *I* help?)

run to the reading—
        forgot the book,
        forgot the time,
forgot the whole dang
DD   MM   YY

*

so perpetually *démodé*,
        so hot,   and SO unable
    to rupture structure

my opprobrium so,
        so so sweaty

*

next up,
        you're stymied
in Seoul,
    apartment-block
birdnest soup farms,
    cave swifts' saliva nests
        collected from ledges

beats beef barbecue onigiri,
    CurioCity food tower,
        ginseng liver schisandra,
infinite digestion

*

interpreting
    this $2 scratchy
is too Oulipo

J Q K = 10
A   = 11

win $4
   minus $2
initial purchase

*

            at last
my dead self
      resurrects,
goes to the hop
   to pitch the woo
   with a bébé tonight

The southern of someplace

is an uncullable guide book,
others bunged
into a grimy skip
out the back
at the besser brick mall
the narcolept's flat out
rough guide open
drooping hand
'the desert begins
just beyond the suburb'
broken hill,
nice type
poliphilus roman
blado italic,
C15th & C16th
respectively.
night stars appear
like the future
like little cysts
like dandruff dust.
my sister's interstices
muttering, muddled,
yet methodical,
hungover, self-conscious,
caught in a laugh trap,
frowning, shuffling,
never standing still,
splinters under skin
a real busy fidget
going places
on the down escalator
passing everyone going up

III

This is what I'm doing at 4 am
FANNY HOWE

Opportunities

Sitting duck
   in Toodyay

add to cart

Lost toy panda
   by the roadside

add to cart

Digital creature,
   crowd-sourced

add to cart

Hearts and minds
   in Oruzgan

add to cart

You're the same age
   as the ugg boot

add to cart

What will tomorrow
   be like

add to cart

If that isn't Dada
   it'll have to do

no further credit

Rehab for Everyone

fingers cold
    tucked under legs,
sitting in insect hiss
    low white noise
gas heater undertone
    no other sound

almost asleep

    a car pulling up the hill

    a currawong
does that shrill thing
    into pink air

a huge open yawn
    almost breaks my jaw

  the pen that makes the marks
    alters the angles of the letters

a patch
    of yesterday's chocolate
      stuck to my corduroy sleeve -
a signal
    imagined and interpreted

we look back
    at the years in the tops
  waiting to be taken out of time

red brick
    wall map of Australia

    grass green carpet
mustard coloured plastic chairs
      clumpy piling on the mittens

mitts on the keyboard
    pushing thoughts and jingles
                out
  to Dublin to Seattle,
    Adelaide, Kane'ohe,
      Faversham, Glebe

sadly notating dim trivia
    me-minus-you
        outside community

literary festivals
    can't help anyone
  like a rehab book sale

making mistakes,
    so different
from being morally wrong

  it's a rabbit life

built the walls
    from Castrol cases

black tyre ribbons
    strewn
  like a giant's licorice
under the striated cutting
    siding on the highway

    say goodbye
           to the Woodford bends

sometimes the clunky
       can incandesce
    but I want to know
how to vitalize gawkiness,

    sometimes
I'm in my no-mind   sometimes
      in a technological mindlessness
sometimes nowhere near limber,
          although that's unusual

some people
      just float along *all* the time
   accumulating the placid

    sometimes
when you think you're going down
        you're not,
you're going straight ahead
          to a utopia of modernity.

Spirulina to go

if you haven't been lost
    at the showground,
in the bush,   in Westfield Plaza,
      on an island

you may not know
      the perpetual present
  is exhausting,

way too many
    concurrent points of view,

—something too <u>free</u> in aleatory—

and further,
    a burden —   a century
  of hortatory Steinisms,
Yes, that's how I read it —

      famously, she says
'a sentence is not emotional, a paragraph is'

the *'difficult'* Stein at her best

  'Think carefully of nouns.
  Vary and think very think very once
  and once more of a noun a noun they like'

DRINKING STRAW — there's your noun, mrs!
    hope you like it

*

discussing Immaculate Conception
        on the landline
&
    Original Sin —
       who *knows* what it is?

   does an individual matter?
         (immeasurable)

*

boys own rumbles by
    on a rusted bicycle
ruining the dawn's bleak dream,
   the flattened one,
     where you emerge from the lake
   and wave, almost languidly

*

there's the dribbling bronze boar
     outside Sydney hospital,
   its snout shiny from stroking

dwelling
   on isolation (don't dwell)
  and other sad feelings (shouldn't dwell)
like a detainee in this,
    the inadequate body

red bumps
   bigger than goosebumps -
but not exactly pimple size
    more weals than whelks

who can understand the nurse
    when she phones
        with the laboratory test data?

*

No one ever here, no footpath crowd,
  every knock of a hinge is creepy
    crack of a floorboard,
        rustle and gust

perhaps it's revelatory,
    or will be

can the past catch up with you

*

problem —   how to begin the music,
      harder than beginning a poem?

the ringtone
    was the sound of that decade

if you just keep turning up
    on time

 eventually

      might rain photons

*

that'd be good

*

you're embarrassed
       by my slurp
when I'm
       guzzling spirulina
          but
I've been to my personal best
       and back —
    I'm not worried

*

early intervention buys time,

how much is time these days?
       (a cheap question)

*

if you see something
       say something—

This is *everything I could want*
       in a lifetime of products

*

pulling on another shirt
    over two shirts
as weather
    sets in

standing in the clothes
      that you once wore

*

hours sitting in one spot

a rosella fell, lodged dead in the branches,
    I took it down
  and buried it behind the begonia

    a new cicada began to chirr

*

I've been coasting,
    a clown visiting a conservatorium,

  time now for application

I want to reach the inhumans,
  find the kind of poetry
    that appeals to them,
to their original intelligence,
  and then,
struck by enargia, Propriety Limited is us

*

Unable to afford
  the G'Day Highway Motel,
I sleep in a car in its shadow

while

the town that makes
  the world's supply
   of plastic drinking straws
 is booming

*

   the dendrite moves slowly
        towards the synapse—
   arrives two weeks later

      WISHING YOU
     A SPEEDY RECOVERY

   the light here is so dim

*

an indestructible host organism
        has the softest touch

strike another match, go start anew

No worries
> *les nouilles ne sont pas toutes dans la soupe*
> *not all the noodles are in the soup*
> (Québecois saying)

flat out,
    too tired to die,

flying across
    the country of soundbites,
 sleeping sitting up
     is impossible
  but
bedroom-eyes slumbers on the aisle,
his casual orange sweater
    emblazoned, kind of gothically,
'Military Order — Devil Dogs'

    *

  real live mesa on the ground
     miles below

Utah,
or maybe Nebraska,

    jet-zone puzzles   like
how IS a mountain formed
  if not volcanically ?

  slow progression

    *

charged-up the camera,
    going on a day tour

pretzel dogs,
  a positive snack discovery

waxed cardboard cups,
    regular means jumbo

      *

all day all night
          on CNN
 tumbling economies

(Baudrillard would have loved
this 'dead cat bounce'
    of stocks & shares)

the Canadian dollar is a 'loony'
  (he'd have liked that too)

      *

up in Québec -
  an actual 'arts constituency'

      *

panhandlers,
  I have to ask,
what's *my* 'social contract'?

      *

exhorted to
    'live better'
yet feeling worse

*

watching a photographer
  conceal himself
behind a column,
    then a curtain
    then a large loud speaker,
now I find him everywhere -
    through a potted palm,
a half empty bookshelf

*

a spotlight catches
    a few silver hairs
      on the back of the neck
of the poet who has been sleeping
through everyone else's reading

*

three empty bottles
  and
how many years have I put into this,
    the meh of z z z z ?

*

from now on
    I will certainly decline

        invitations to travel far,
I'll never see China, for instance

           I don't really mind
   not seeing anywhere

I'll meander
        around some bend
  like Lucky & Pozzo,
    arrive from nowhere
    make a speech
      and leave

        only half genuine,
you disappear before you're gone

    no worries

Leaving the World

is not as bad
as you'd think

the grand movement
masks
the small movement,
you pull your swifty
and disappear

*

now in the habit
of taking evil
in your stride,
(thanks to you,
    US drones)

five years after the day
you shrouded
the Guernica replica

you find you have
no further questions

for the time being

along the LA freeway
black derricks
trundle up and down
like
Jean Tinguely sculptures,
only   ominous

& witless
in a waterless world

*

we would like to clear
the trees,
enable the panorama

no longer photograph
the coloured leaves
tourists come to see

*

men make man made,
you can study them
making memoir
under the summit

eat up big,
feed your hero,
poke him,
could become Pegasus,
born from Picasso's wound

*

the way
he never leaves himself
alone

and always
disregards The Real

*

he drank
crystal-infused water
all night long, for nights on end,
then
placed his body on a bed
and went out of the room

Living

too much jazz and shouting cuban
    in the greyest dark of day
when you simply want to wallow

turning cold to kiddy colours—
    their popular difficulties
and bright individual conventions

wiping out obliquities
    you can't ever be cool,
plus, capital has failed you, properly

failure dogs your genre too,
    the ciphers in the lines
refuse conceptual interpretations

keychains and bushranger beards
    pose, stovepiped, in seminars,
unravelling new idiom, new new

mothy inkblots are a cult hit,
    complacency is no fun
but it is, in your case, restful

sceptical optimism—a phrase that jars
    as it claims its triumph
like plastic's morbid persistence

atmosphere's leaden now you've said that,
    done and gone, poorly,
nothing left marvellous, only living

Haywire here

who prepared this future?

*

    I know
not every poem
      needs to be clever
e.g.
      pigeon follows woman
      on missenden road

*

a mere minute harbourside
      convinces me
that three years
      of bleak heath
    is way too long—

when a day is grey
    it's a boring day

and the barmaid's
   never heard of sarsaparilla

(worse for me
    & you)

but Sydney,
  city of humidity & hail,
  never
      WENT AWAY

I fell into
   its failing, messy, smoggy,
      shoving 'unsustainability' often,

I wiped spoons
      on a tea towel map
of the dysfunctional transport system

after riding back
   on a train filled with rubbish.

I missed
   the annual rock star slide projections
         on Utzon's tiles

missed lemon granita
         and a few four star movies

also,
  I spent a long time
    remembering
         how great it is—
  a harbour dip
      beneath bloated clouds

*

whatever it's like
      anywhere,   here

this treble clef
    transfers energy,
an exact exchange

   (keep the score)

    the semi-quaver
        is improvised

    any percussion?

    red beans
      splatter
          all over the bench
    (pastry cook howling)

    *

    whatever it's like
        in somewhere world
    it's really haywire here

        *

    wrapping the heavy rugs
            in plastic

    we lug them down
      down
        to the nuns' coal cellar
          under the house

        ungainly

    like
      Penelope Cruz in 'Volver'
        getting the body
      to the restaurant freezer

    *

napping's
    what I want to do

sleep
  is my *mise en scène,*

preferring
 weather forecasts
     to poems

did you say 'drudgery'?
  no, I said
     'drugsery'

*

taste buds quelled
    from the glue
on the sympathy card envelope

*

poets perceive language
    directly

*

 'the *I* never thinks of itself
as an effect'
 yet
    I move my shadow
  across your eyes
     inventing a new expression

*

    haven't been outside
             today

       window

   snow showers
      swirl onto windscreens

go so low,
       low and slow

water trickles
   from the roof corner
onto a sopping
      firetail finch

*

outside in a way
    anyway

IV

I have always lived close
to the television
        GREGORZ WRÓBLEWSKI

Dry ice

this is the place to come,
    to work in winter in summer,
it's in a photo of shadows—

staring out at the rain
    that's always falling
    from the poetry magazine skies

the people in this archive
      know how to be quiet,
  plugging in
    to the table sockets,
lining up to hot spots

  (but
why are the reference shelves
    empty
      from 495 - 580,
  from south asia to botany?)

it's way above
      the traffic,   no birds,
  a fake pot plant, specks of diesel
      on the upwind,
too noisy to sit outside,
  too high up to stand and lean
(resist a chronic urge
    to throw yourself over the railing,
  splat onto the white double lines—
a broken up bloodied blob,
        finished)
maybe safer
  to use the hi-speed internet

            at Woolworths,
    no balcony there

                *

in the evening,
        under a windstorm,
watching Alfred Hitchcock's 'Sabotage'
    needles and pills in the cooler,
            (none for pleasure),
contemplating decomposing
            (an elegy for complications)
        in a lull in the drama

                *

Georges Bataille said
    By writing I wanted to get to the bottom of things.
    And, having given myself this task, I fell asleep.

                *

'no content, only dirt'
        Linh Dinh podcasts.
I am at your front door, Linh,
    it's early,
  garbage trucks make their hyperaubade,
            I'd like to contribute
but I wouldn't know
        bad junk from good junk

same problems in poems, poetry magazines,
    news sites, plays, sciences, films—
            and I'm fuming like dry ice,

can poetry do it though,
      specifically, address problems
            from the sofa,
when the world erupts
      in high definition,
   dictatorships crack and collapse,
  corporate investment implodes,
            can't poetry follow ?

        *

eyes narrow, lids lost their spring -
      there's no spring in your lid these days,
  just like Bataille, falling asleep.

down below
   globs of gobspit dot the bitumen,
mesmerised, up here,
      by the pulsing glow of standby
  lighting a narcotic path
         to the Foxtel card slot

Seriously
for Susan Schultz

only some theories
are conspiracies
and where regular
means giant
regular means giant

it's just
circumstantial evidence
that gives validity
to the main behaviour
of metro cosmo
politans
and their
convoluted elegies

and then
it does take time
to remember 'simile',
though
'analogy' is there,
in the foreground

photo op's
now 'pic fac',
(something you'd
appreciate)
picture facility
manipulated
photoshopped

I thought of
'furtive shame'

too
but could never say it
as well as you

in this situation
canned laughter
does my laughing
for me

watching
'To Be Advised'
again,
the world
is becoming
the same place

A moving cloud

something daily
    crops up
        (every day)

opening the front door
    to look out
        at the spreading light
and blue, green, some grey
        and a stripey bird,
there's
    a brown packet
        folded to fit the letter box,
a tube of yellow and red
    junk mail
        fixed on the flaky railing
between dark green palings

    *

walking everywhere
        on my birthday,
  after a haircut
        at 'New Do',
a kind of gamine cut
        for older persons
  (I like to think)

    the sky, so active,
a fast moving cloud here
        a jet fuel stream over there
another streakier cloud
        and a luminous sun

'New Do'
    could have been
decorated
  with what Conrad called
    'those homosexual home essentials'
but, thankfully,
      it's plain in there
  and friendly,
    no frills, no furbelows

    *

and you know what?
  I decide, <u>yes</u>—
    today I'll make a dash
towards the <u>new</u>
  on a warm and yellowy
  oosporic autumn day,
    just this once

I'll do
something *different*
  to celebrate
    getting as old as this
beneath the moving clouds

    *

plugged in,
    as I go along,
to a slippery fish of a singer

    *

interstate planes,
    red and grey and orange,
  womble overhead
      going north

soft and fast,
  a plane shadow
     crosses the path
like an electrical brownout

    *

I'm thinking,
    as I tread the trail,
of today's Melbourne poets—
poets
   at truth's drinking fountain

born ninety kilometres
  up the road
 in an insignificant town called Seymour
(sorry, Seymouresian people,
   I hope things have changed for you)
near
  Puckapunyal military camp,
I was a young Melbournian once,
    on my motorbike
    in the later '70s' zany years

    *

  at Broadway
in the 'photo-me' booth
   I adjust the stool
     by spinning it up

and notice a spent bandaid
    on the floor

four flashes,
    alive in sight for a split-second,
        are blinding,
the photos aren't any good

    *

living near the airport
    worrying
        anything rattling
            up in the sky
is something wrong

    *

Melbourne poets of today
        hello!

I had a spam message
    from 'Art Institutes'
        (whoever *they* are)
subject:
    'Design a New Future for Yourself'

    (sounds good to me)

        what do you think?

    *

when I showed you
    Eileen's phone poem—

        'phone isn't
        the same string
        from person to
        person now
        that we carry
        them and
        have no homes'
 you smiled
    appreciatively
to yourself
    and   said
mid-'70s
    telephone trees
were
   precursors
to mobile phone
      revolutions

    *

on the edge
    of the city map
 the airport
      smothers the bay—
like a fat blue
     bulging
  pigeon-toed pathogen

    *

last week
  I caught a plane to Adelaide

a number of passengers
    carried flat white cardboard boxes

    of sugary sweet, smooth, iced
        Krispy Kreme doughnuts
not
    anything like
proper slightly lumpy golden doughnuts
        i.e. REAL doughnuts

    aeroplane performance art

don't they *have*
    Krispy Kreme
        in Adelaide?

      *

    on the ground here,
in the distance
    at the top
        of the sky
    super-white contrails stretch up
above
    an orange and brown pile driver
lodged in the middle
        of a muddy construction site

(and no driver)

    walking back now,
I did
    nothing *different*

(and no photos)

      *

   remember all those years here
                when
                          World Square
  was a grand square
             cavity in the ground
after the developer
                went to jail

and,   nearby,
   meeting
       Slim Dusty
  in the EMI
             recording studio
  next to the giant gulping
       eight-storey parking station
in Castlereagh Street,
  Slim kept
his big brimmed bush hat
     on
        all the time

In my phone
for Gig Ryan

you said we didn't but we did
   have telephones
      in late seventies' share houses,
bulky bakelite telephones
   ringing as often
      as Frank O'Hara's
and Brigid Berlin's did, a decade earlier

we had honour systems—
   add phone calls
      to a running total
in a column under your name,
like a boardgame score,
     pay up
when the household bill arrives

   *

I could ring to say
   sometimes I imagine you
in a Max Ernst collage
      (*Une semaine de bonté*)

there's a woman reflected
   in an ornately gilded mirror
      behind an open door,
you're the other woman
   guiding a feathered bird-man
   into a high Edwardian
      drawing room—
he carries a tooled leather bag,
   he seems to be a doctor,

"mind how you go doctor" you say
   "just step over
      the apoplectic monkey, doctor"

doctor feathered bird-man
      brings sleeping elixir,
  an anodyne

          *

in sleep
      I'm filled with thought,
my dream constructed
      not by surrealism
          but by Slabs R Us,
solid, solemn, grey

half asleep, half dreaming,
   a phone is ringing,
      I hold the earpiece close—
friends pollute the swoony hours
      with caring

in a poetry world
  everything is providential,
      or not,
and, sometimes,
    just life on hold, call waiting,
  like Tennyson's poetic

reading now, quiet,
      a newer title—
  I always skip
    redacted poems,
the crossings-out seem obvious

and attention seeking—
you would agree?
      your number's in my phone,
I could call to ask.

Nina Hagen

        (once
        upon
        a time)

nineteen hundred sixty-eight is over
    is flimsy politics
  pummeled, disconnected,
diachronicity
    indicating
technology's noisy cataclysm
& flashing strobe
      boxed in a dusty garage

nineteen hundred ninety-eight is over
    is how to scratch
  the future
      when it's gone,
  thinking pastness
       is up ahead

twenty oh eight is over
    is atmospheric brooding,
  interpretation rules
  the day, the weeks,
      years, the centuries

(sliding in
    to hide beneath
the warmth of flock and shoddy,
  ruffling
    dust in the circuitry)

twenty ten
    is nothing else—

laser beam a pilot's eyes,
        upstage an apocalypse,
my ten cent technophile
    you're in my echo chamber,
        my feedback loop

twenty thirteen
    is corporately social, filtered,
nothing deviant here,
      hop away now, recharge,
  unencumbered
    &
      unapologetic

Nina — it's all big data,
      an entry in a ledger

What's the frequency, Kenneth?

a revhead full of vodka slushies,
      fading bling, the schlock of the old.
just don't hand over the car keys.

sampling a fizz of schweppervescence
  I think of us, you and me,
      our lifetime lack of fancy salaries.
on a close and muggy morning
  I muddled a muddled job interview,
      their risible enquiries,
my irrelevant,
    yet *innovative*, projects,
          dah de dah

*

walking up through Erskineville
  the florist's mauve-tinged cabbages
      remind me of Derek Jarman
and of a lover who stayed indoors
  drawing plants
      for years,
funny to think it now
  but when she said it was agoraphobia
    I visited her darkened flat
    and gave her all my Neil Young records.

*

I wonder how it is for you, this instant,
    like,   today,
at your four days a week job,
      a cluttered counter—

papers, keyboard, pencils,
        'On The Level Everyday'
stacked beside something intense, like
      'Living in the End Times',
guarding a small corner of sapient activity
(sounds pretentious,
      though to me, true)
charged with bearing, mien,
not temporal,
      more the neurons' frenzied,
although private, oscillations,
      that some groover might call 'vibes',
going as fast as
      or faster than
        the Giant Hadron Collider
zzzzmmmmmm zzzzmmmmmm zzzzmmmmmm
in the government-funded
      intellectual art world

or

casual days, loafing with art theory,
worrying only that the bright summer light
      might pierce the shopfront windows,
and fade the display

my memorylessness—
      which direction does the building face?

      *

something lacklustre about
    lacking lustre
        like the squarest greyest

block of apartments
 always called 'Liberty'

   *

anyway
  I feel it
   going to my very shivering, clicking
    axiological bones,
that palpitating measure, (*what she say?*
    what she mean?)
  that you have going there,
       art critic.

Closed on Mondays

        too nice
  &   when you leave

everything is white noise,
      no traffic,
no music,   no muffle,
  just thick air
        whirring

greyness leaks
    into the afternoon,
a dirty kind of day

kids are rolling
    down a mound
      of irradiated tilth

the world's
    assembled curatariat
is queuing unhappily
     for their passes
  in light drizzle

perdido's
   on eastside
& I'm trying ballerina moves
    on the fibre mat,
  preceding biceps curls
with pitiful
     one kilogram weights

a tiny plastic 'T'
   snipped from

        a price tag,
caught in the mat

is there any
     news from Mars
that's better
        than here?

      *

latest is
   R.Mutt's a meme

it was when you said
" say
   'thanks Marcel' "

      *

death's announced
   to
     a quick declivity
        (joke)
of upload, list & link—
scrolling,
    the final ritual

mourners weeping,
    for themselves,
no ghost
 in the crematorium machine

      *

    like Georges Perec wrote—
        Nothing is happening, in fact

every single thing's
    a tourist destination
&
  everything's
      available to everyone

taking phone photos
    of the brickworks stacks
from the back seat
    on saturday night

gawking at the mud
    caked on cars
drifting
    on the flood plain

      *

time experienced
  as a perpetual rush
    to
      the latest in new

o no
    it's Monday
it's closed

& you reveal
    a dour scepticism
        of pop culture
  but
I'd give it
    another chance

following
     my dorky polestar,
relentlessly discursive

        *

     open the cider

  'thanks Marcel'

       *

so you want
     to write in a cave
        &
take your source material
     with you?

      *

searching all over
    for the house
      where it's quiet
    because
Wallace Stevens
      says it is

     *

a vase
   of droopy roses

fine dust covering
     a tower
   of expended
      nivea cream jars

*

&
    when I arrive
        there's a manuscript,
   poems,   new to me,
open for reading

    the first pages
       have
          draft numbers—
Draft #1 Draft #2
            —at the top

before anything else
      the rims around
 my eyes
     feel tired

the empty room
      purrs its scope

I imagine
  a well-polished
        furniture voice
trying nonchalance,
    the sheets of typing
          called
  " my stuff "

*

it's coming along

*

   stretch out now,
      a woven plastic lounge

   muscle & bone grind
      shoulder bone
         grind

   warm your dead feet
      beneath the baobab tree

         *

thin transparent oil
        slowly leaks
  from the barrel
     of the souvenir pen,
the plastic historical figure
    no longer slides
   along the mini city backdrop,
      he's stuck
at the bottom of the scene

         *

mid april
  &
     the xmas wreath
is still pinned
   to the front door
     of the neighbour
who died
   on boxing day

V

I don't want to work I want to smoke
                        GUILLAUME APOLLINAIRE

Worldless

where's my donkey :   thursday evening

catch the train,
      seagulls circling
           Central Station

catch a bus
     pick up a paint chart,

at the gallery—
     Korea and Kinglake
         photography exhibitions

     (different)

a very thin man
   in Oxford Street
      in red leather pants

talk on Eastside Radio
     read two poems

at the bus stop
     long haired boys—
regenerate fashion,
   retro,
fashions
  arrive & go by
    really quickly—
I had to live through
     the entire decades!

    (peeved)

catch a bus,
    redhead woman driver
playing jazz piano cd
      loudly, in the bus
   (suits the traffic)

catch the train,
  seagulls gone to Pyrmont,
night workers
   eating chocolates & chips

    (hunger)

walk to the seafood shop
   buy the dory, grilled

    walk home

     *

I am the donkey : saturday afternoon

step onto the crossing,
   lift palm to car,
  thanks driver.
quicken pace, cross smartly,
think
   'why do I do that
   why do I want to live
   am I depressed?'

Scottish sentimentality—
   car alarm with violin

    (answer)

*

I pass the donkey : tuesday morning

walk to the bus stop
    (forgot my watch & silver ring)
   open umbrella,
      light rain shower

catch the sad bus
   through the streets
     around
   sad blocks of flats

paint swatches
  (I must remember)

what colour the door?
  the brick fence, what colour?

coffee at Zoo,
    hair colour in the arcade
   (regrowth)

buy underwear,
   blue, mauve,
    & stripey

buy preserving jar
   (lemons)

buy
   honey, celtic sea salt
     & iodised sea salt

carrot & celery juice,
the juice maker
   takes ages
  to juice the vegetables

almost miss the bus

quickly buy the newspaper,
   here's the bus

winding back
  past Centennial Park

there's the donkey,
  no, it's a horse

  (mistaken)

here are the streets
  around
 the sad flats
   & here's
the Cauliflower Hotel

listen to Patti Smith 'Twelve'
 (Changing of the Guards!)
  on an ipod
    on the bus

on the move
  but in the clouds

  (worldless)

    thought stuck,
        pinned down

    stupid under
      a roaring sky

         *

there is no donkey : friday night

hazard lights
  in the bus lane

police
    remove the number plate,
the driver
    brays drunkenly
      (caught)

going home
  to make a poem
(this one)
    to give my problems
to you, reader

    (contagion)

everything fails
    when all else fails,
        when all else
    skyrockets

some of what I think
    is a piece of crap

some of what I know
           is worse

some things I say
      shouldn't be said

my heart,
    meaning
  my feelings towards you,
        reader,
meaning
   my straight ahead empathy,
      though
  is
    in the right place

nearly home,
   the streets seem dark

enter the house,
       hug you,
my synthetic coat
      squeaks

Feed the orchid

says the note
near the radio,
tuning in to
New Weird Australia,
dangle a tea bag
into a mug,
anticipate
sound sounds
experiment, montage,
batteries flat,
dance on nothing,
have to go
suck a stone
instead.
measuring up
sight unseen
sound unheard,
dogged continuum—
swallow the algae,
long for the moss,
fondle the root,
a wasp hovers
over a corn cob,
wasp or bee?
makes me think
of Maeterlinck,
Count Maurice
Maeterlinck,
his second name
was Polydore,
original
in countless ways—
his never-made

Metro Goldwyn Mayer
movie   based on
'The Life of the Bee'.
is this a
sappy nature poem?
notate imperilled
imperilling plants,
vanishing insects,
the superseded
cochineal beetle.
missing grasses,
what weed
is that ?
too bad about
the prickly pear.

iNext twilight

here comes my grim counterpart,
(not my twin), choose an orange or lime
high visibility vest, speak through
a computer, explain length in time.
twilighting a remix age,
swirling galaxy giveaways
fill the box, no strings,
stick a decal on your helmet.
vault down a worm hole,
get going quickly,
avoid the frothy quantum spume,
message cowpowder and sashes ashes,
go on, take the bilious-looking vest.

All fuelled out

watercolour's a riddle, the city
fucked-up & not like Paris,
watery suburbs as watery depictions,
like a Raoul Dufy biscuit box lid
or Emil Nolde slumped over chips,
pommes frites to the ornamental bugger
who pecks and putts his flirty air kisses
towards your coral aquarelles.
doodling on the bubbled backs
of soaked-off claret labels, sunk
into a bucket of silence.

A day late

rough idle,
  dirty spark plugs,
 slept in,
  bitten
  by an abstract insect,
a day late

excuses fold
  into a blush
   of predictability
as if
  after last, next
    and one more,
 there's only one kind of time

no gauche forays
  into the underglot,
you're home by dark
  with a box of wine

moving the bricks around,
  from one bump
   to another,
 your little portable cosmogony,
how similar it is
  to an algorithm
 you gave up on
    years ago

the way you felt
  on the long way round
and what you thought
  you smelled—

   acrid air
       at the monument factory
  and what you saw there—
         a riddle
 to snare
     some imaginary solution

Sugar tube

out of the ordinary
erroneous blood

smoking head

but everything's
still linear

and

hail is always
the size of golfballs.

when was it
contaminated

and

why
were you there?

flirting with solipsism
take a second look

we would like you
to participate

because

it's fun and rewarding

take
liberties

take up
the offer.

don't be so
sanguine

blue blood
on your hands

it's all there
in the assay.

a tube of sugar

please

free
radical scavenger

like dub pop
hope

maybe

but

those yellow zinnias
in the sand
aren't as tall
as they were.
since when does a flower
grow shorter in two weeks?

under the glary
rare earth scandium light

oxydised cat food

and

no kitty

the hot colours
of the plastic
laundry product bottles.

sentinel,
did you
have a say?

More than a feuilleton

the experienced world
  hasn't been
      the world itself
for a long time
      now

& now   we want
  to see the world
     as we want it to be

      *

who's speaking,
     saying this
   about the 'world' ?
what 'world' ?

      *

a cute commodity
   nestles
    in my indifferent hand
as
   I bend, or bow, really,
to sniff
   a savoury crush
     of peppermint and sage

a torn canvas awning flaps
      in slow motion,
the herbicide's
   left dripping

on the fronds,
it's picturesque, I suppose

*

can't call the sentimental
'sentimental'
when it's very moving

the next step
is to explain it

the way you can
'lose your self'
to a tear,
to a tremble even,
whenever *that* song
begins,
when *that* scent
wafts —
a prelude
to loss, to getting lost

*

seeking a way
back—
incapable
of turning to the classics
or history?

a minor chronicler
of moments?

hey, stop.

I *googled*
  actaeon,

erechtheion
  I've never seen.

   I know the picture,
  plus the concept
 of the caryatids
    (writing that line
  way back—
    'carrying you out
      like a caryatid'),
were they strong or subservient?

  hard to tell
    with a building
  on your back

didn't even
    thumb the index
  of Larousse mythology!

    *

a certain lassitude
  in completing
    the research
is not that funky

  but

everythin' I do
  gonna be funky
  from now on

126

*

    maybe
   leap
  drop
   slip and slide
   like a penguin
      on antarctic ice

*

over hoaxes

the trick
   is
de-anonymisation,

get
  'better known'
is that what's needed ?

   doubt it

*

and the truth is scant

*

my week
   is my weekend

my task—
   reinvigorate ossified poetries
  by adulteration

involve
        the 'always' factor—

arguments
    are always
            a social event

boredom
    is always
counter-revolutionary. always.
    (Guy Debord
        allows himself
            a double 'always'
& so he should)

who says 'penned'
    instead of
        'wrote' or 'written'?
always say
 I *data entered*
        that poem!

                *

middle of the dark night
    news—
suicide bombing
            in Damascus
police teargas thousands
            in Homs

messages from 2010lab.tv
            in Dortmund
and galatea resurrects
            in California

  google galatea
    or go back to bed?

  no need,
   you already know
    that marble revenant

  click on the link
   or leave until morning?

  sleep the computer
    feel your way
     in night shadows,
   bump the bulky lounge chair,
  bare feet
    follow the rug edge,

     the bedroom

  the bed

    *

  the world
    dreamed,
  no better than
    as is

    *

  who's that
   saying this
    about the 'world'?

    *

hard to believe
        now
            but
every age will be lamented,
            even this one

heard that
        somewhere

Acknowledgements

Some of these poems, sometimes in different versions, were published in *Cordite, Cultural Studies Review, ETZ, Fieralingue, foam:e, Heat, Island, Otoliths, Overland, Parthenon West Review, Pinstripe Fedora, Rabbit, Southerly, Steamer, The Age, The Best Australian Poems 2010, 2011* and *2012, THIS Corner, VLAK,* and *AU/UA: Contemporary Poetry of Ukraine and Australia,* as part of the digital experiment *WOW WOW WOW RECEIVER, A Poetic Intervention* at Frankfurt Book Fair, Germany, 2011, in the e-book *the meh of z z z z* (Ahadada, 2010), and in the chapbooks *Anyworld* (Flying Island, 2012) and *More than a feuilleton* (Little Esther, 2012).

A few lines and phrases in this collection are inherited or altered from Daniel Levin Becker, Joshua Clover, Rachel Blau DuPlessis, Kenward Elmslie, Eileen Myles, Vanessa Place, Joan Retallack, Iain Sinclair, Juliana Spahr, Jack Spicer, Gertrude Stein and John Tranter.

In 'American Memories, Melbourne'—the quote from the 'Famous American Female Poet' is from 'Above The Leaders' by Alice Notley (Veer Books, 2008) and the 'yellow zinnias' stanza in 'Sugar tube' is from Alfred Hitchcock's film *Rear Window*.

In 'A day late'—'little portable cosmogony' is the title of Raymond Queneau's verse tour of human knowledge *Petite cosmogonie portative*.

The title 'What's the frequency, Kenneth?' is a song by the alternative rock group R.E.M. from their 1994 album *Monster*. The phrase 'What's the frequency, Kenneth?' has connotations in the USA that can be left to Wikipedia to explicate. Its use here is entirely benign, affectionate even.

www.ingramcontent.com/pod-product-compliance
Lightning Source LLC
Chambersburg PA
CBHW031153160426
43193CB00008B/347